PLAY IN THE AGE OF GOETHE

NEW STUDIES IN THE AGE OF GOETHE

New Studies in the Age of Goethe, sponsored by the Goethe Society of North America, aims to publish innovative research that contextualizes the "Age of Goethe," whether within the fields of literature, history (including art history and history of science), philosophy, art, music, or politics. Though the series editors welcome all approaches and perspectives, they are especially interested in interdisciplinary projects, creative approaches to archival or original source materials, theoretically informed scholarship, work that introduces previously undiscovered materials, and projects that re-examine traditional epochal boundaries or open new channels of interpretations.

TITLES IN THE SERIES

Edgar Landgraf and Elliott Schreiber, eds., *Play in the Age of Goethe: Theories, Narratives, and Practices of Play around 1800*

Ellwood Wiggins, *Odysseys of Recognition: Performing Intersubjectivity in Homer, Aristotle, Shakespeare, Goethe, and Kleist*

Seán Williams, *Pretexts for Writing: German Romantic Prefaces, Literature, and Philosophy*

Vance Byrd, *A Pedagogy of Observation: Nineteenth-Century Panoramas, German Literature, and Reading Culture*

Christine Lehleiter, *Romanticism, Origins, and the History of Heredity*

Benjamin Bennett, *Aesthetics as Secular Millennialism: Its Trail from Baumgarten and Kant to Walt Disney and Hitler*

Mary Helen Dupree, *The Mask and the Quill: Actress-Writers in Germany from Enlightenment to Romanticism*

Peter J. Schwartz, *After Jena: Goethe's Elective Affinities and the End of the Old Regime*

Brian Tucker, *Reading Riddles: Rhetorics of Obscurity from Romanticism to Freud*

PLAY IN THE AGE OF GOETHE

Theories, Narratives, and Practices of Play around 1800

Edited by Edgar Landgraf and Elliott Schreiber

Bucknell University | University Press
Lewisburg, Pennsylvania

Library of Congress Cataloging-in-Publication Data

Names: Landgraf, Edgar, 1967- editor. | Schreiber, Elliott, 1969- editor.
Title: Play in the age of Goethe: theories, narratives, and practices of play around 1800 / edited by Edgar Landgraf and Elliott Schreiber.
Description: Lewisburg, Pennsylvania: Bucknell University Press, [2020] | Series: New studies in the age of Goethe | Includes bibliographical references and index.
Identifiers: LCCN 2019043878 | ISBN 9781684482061 (paperback) | ISBN 9781684482078 (cloth) | ISBN 9781684482085 (epub) | ISBN 9781684482092 (mobi) | ISBN 9781684482108 (pdf)
Subjects: LCSH: Play—Psychological aspects—History—18th century. | Play—Psychological aspects—History—19th century. | Play—Social aspects—History—18th century. | Play—Social aspects—History—19th century.
Classification: LCC BF717 .P5764 2020 | DDC 306.4/81—dc23
LC record available at https://lccn.loc.gov/2019043878

A British Cataloging-in-Publication record for this book is available from the British Library.

∞ The paper used in this publication meets the requirements of the American National Standard for Information Sciences—Permanence of Paper for Printed Library Materials, ANSI Z39.48-1992.

www.bucknelluniversitypress.org

Distributed worldwide by Rutgers University Press

Manufactured in the United States of America

CONTENTS